Mary & Sit too

I hope you will enjoy this little book. Many thanks for the food you brought to us over the years. Also thanks for taking me to Mass when Ron was in rehab. Also thank you for your friendship.

Love You,
Colleen + Ron

D0863644

I KNOW GOD IS ALIVE
He's in My Kitchen

SUE HUSTON

WESTBOW
PRESS®
A DIVISION OF THOMAS NELSON
& ZONDERVAN

Scripture taken from the King James Version of the Bible.

This book is a work of non-fiction. Unless otherwise noted, the author and the publisher make no explicit guarantees as to the accuracy of the information contained in this book and in some cases, names of people and places have been altered to protect their privacy.

WestBow Press books may be ordered through booksellers or by contacting:

WestBow Press
A Division of Thomas Nelson & Zondervan
1663 Liberty Drive
Bloomington, IN 47403
www.westbowpress.com
1 (866) 928-1240

Because of the dynamic nature of the Internet, any web addresses or links contained in this book may have changed since publication and may no longer be valid. The views expressed in this work are solely those of the author and do not necessarily reflect the views of the publisher, and the publisher hereby disclaims any responsibility for them.

Any people depicted in stock imagery provided by Thinkstock are models, and such images are being used for illustrative purposes only.
Certain stock imagery © Thinkstock.

ISBN: 978-1-5127-1915-4 (sc)
ISBN: 978-1-5127-1917-8 (hc)
ISBN: 978-1-5127-1916-1 (e)

Library of Congress Control Number: 2015919003

Print information available on the last page.

WestBow Press rev. date: 12/09/2015

CONTENTS

ENDORSEMENTS

"As a child, I knew Sue Huston to be one of the kindest, most loving grown-ups in my life. She was fantastic at telling the stories my friends and I needed to hear. As an adult, I'm thrilled to see her applying her thoughtful, grace-filled perspective to these tales of parenting struggles, answered prayers, and God's provision. The stories in the book may be exactly what you need to hear, too."

Jason Boyett, author of *O Me of Little Faith*

"I had the privilege and honor of serving with Sue Huston as a colleague and her pastor. I found her to be a wonderful example of the love of Jesus Christ, not just in words, but in action and deed, as well. She has a caring heart for all people. Sue lives the Christian faith and has a wonderful impact on all around her. She lives a life of prayer."

Don Reed, retired minister

"You will thoroughly enjoy these inspirational quick reads. The stories are just long enough to bring a breath of fresh air to a stressful day when we have not taken time to offer gratitude or thanks to Him."

Amy Baker, Superintendent of Schools

ACKNOWLEDGMENTS

Heartfelt thanks to Kristi Horine, whose editorial expertise was invaluable to me. I'm grateful to David Snell, Connie Thane, Carolyn Coons, and my Writers' Group for reading and listening to the stories over and over and offering suggestions for improvement.

Constance Beauman provided the ideas for the cover design, and Dennis Hinkle was kind enough to make me look respectable for the author's photograph.

DEDICATION

For my children, the joys of my life. They have kept me on my toes and on my knees. And for my husband Price, whose loving support has been a blessing throughout our years together. I love them all dearly.

PREFACE

"God is great,
God is good,
Let us thank Him for our food."

"Now I lay me down to sleep;
I pray the Lord my soul to keep.
If I should die before I wake
I pray the Lord my soul to take."

I love to pray. I loved the repeated prayers I learned in my early childhood. It was exciting when I realized I could add some of my own words to those verses: God bless Mommy, God bless Daddy, God bless my sister, God bless Granny, God bless Uncle Carey, God bless the dog and the cat, God blesses the hamster; and the list went on. Then my mother taught me, mostly by her example, to include specific needs in my prayers. "Let's ask God to make Granny's knee feel better," she might suggest. Or maybe she would pray, "Dear Lord, help Aunt Joy find a job that she will enjoy."

By my teen years, my conversations with God reflected a greater awareness of His love and power. And through the years, my prayer life has become more and more meaningful and important in my day to day walk with God. Those of us who have known the Lord from childhood can probably track our spiritual growth by the kinds of prayers we offered during the seasons of our lives.

The sincere prayers of children are precious to me. In our Sunday school prayer time, first grader Julie thanked God for Jesus and for the Bible. Then she went further saying, "Now God, you know that me and Billy don't have no mommy and Betsy don't have no daddy. Now God, you got to take care of us…." I believe with all my heart that God answered her prayer and continues to answer it as she grows.

Through the years I documented many experiences in which God answered my prayers positively or otherwise. I also collected stories about answered prayer that friends, family members and acquaintances shared with me.

This book is a compilation of some of those experiences and stories. They have taken place over a span of many years, but each of them is a special memory and proof of God's abiding care.

It is my sincere prayer that you, the reader, will be reminded of God's power and love as you identify with one or more of the situations described in the book. May your faith be reinforced and your prayer life strengthened by the experiences of others.

In some cases names have been changed.

Scriptures are from the King James Version of the Bible.

PART 1

In My Kitchen

CHAPTER 1

Decisions, Decisions

When I am faced with the prospect of decision making, my mind goes directly to the place where many evaluations and determinations in my life were made: – the kitchen. In particular, the kitchen table.

The earliest decisions I can remember were not mine, but they concerned me and had a great deal to do with my well- or not-so-well-being. They were made at my mother's kitchen table.

At age four I sat very straight with my hands in my lap. My mother was sitting across from me sobbing uncontrollably. She was saying to my father, seated at the end of the table, "It'll take a whole year! I know it! A whole year!" Then she turned to me and, for the fourth time, asked through her tears, "My precious little girl, how could you do this to me?"

I remember trying to understand how cutting off my own curly bangs at the scalp was doing something "to my mother." However, I had enough presence of mind not to voice my thoughts. And, these many years later, having been a mother, my understanding of those words is crystal clear.

That particular day, there were two decisions to be made at the table: a. how to fix me to look presentable by Sunday morning and, b. what disciplinary action would be appropriate for my transgression. I had learned in Sunday School that God is always with us and hears us when we pray. I strongly sensed that this was the time to call upon Him, earnestly and silently, right there at the kitchen table. Though, I do not recall my exact words, my prayer probably was something like, "Help! Help!" How my mother managed to make me presentable escapes my memory, but I do remember the swatting I got from my father!

Did God answer my prayer? Yes. He answered it in the way that would benefit me the most, even though it was not the answer I was hoping for.

Years later, at the same table, the decision under consideration was whether or not I would be allowed to go out with a boy who was a high school dropout, had his own car, a leather jacket and a questionable reputation. In my sophomore opinion he was *sooo* neat! As I think back on it, he was the spitting image of Fonzie– a cool dude on a current television series. I pointed out that I could probably convince him to come to church with us sometime. Now think about it. Wouldn't you think that most parents would be happy for their daughter to have the opportunity to have a date with Fonzie and be a Christian witness at the same time? But, no! Not my mother!

This time, I was the one who sobbed uncontrollably and said, "How could you do this to me?" And my mother was the one who prayed silently. Again God answered. I did live through the disappointment and later thanked her for her decision.

In time, I acquired my own kitchen table, which came to be the site of more decisions and a host of family conferences. The prayers offered there were often pleas for help for myself or for others. There were prayers of intercession and prayers for wisdom, strength and guidance. It surely must be a rare parent who can rear a family without a kitchen table!

＝≡≡＝

Be careful for nothing; but in everything by prayer
and supplication with thanksgiving let your requests
be made known unto God: And the peace of
God, which passeth all understanding shall keep
your hearts and minds through Christ Jesus.

Phllippians 4:6-7

＝≡≡＝

CHAPTER 2

A Grieving Daughter

The kitchen table has also been the site of my personal Bible study and the setting for many heart-to-heart sessions with friends. Often I received encouragement or advice, and sometimes the conversation centered on the person across from me - a grieving friend, a lonely neighbor, or someone who needed a listening ear.

Betty, a young mother, was deep in grief over the loss of her own mother to cancer. Betty had pleaded with the Lord to destroy the malignant cells and bring healing to her loved one. "I have always counted on Mother's help in raising my children," she sobbed. "I need her advice, her experience and her patience to guide me through the years to come." But God had taken the saintly grandmother to be with Him in heaven.

The precious bond that had existed between the mother and daughter was difficult to release. Praying aloud, I asked the Lord to make His presence very real to this brokenhearted friend. I prayed for a healthy period of grief, knowing that God understands our deepest hurts and guides us through our pains and sorrows to reach the ultimate peace He offers.

The memorial service, the burial, and the comforting friends became a blur. Betty's husband graciously took over the care of the children for a while, even though he, too, felt the pain of losing one he loved.

Weeks passed before Betty could say, "I'm doing better." Months passed before Betty could say, "I'm not angry at God anymore." Then the day came when she entered my kitchen with a smile on her face and said, "God has shown me that He did answer my prayers. He did, indeed, heal my mother! He gave her a brand-new body with no pain and no weaknesses."

As she continued, we learned that God had also made it plain to her that He would provide everything she needed to raise her children in the nurture and admonition of the Lord. Already she had met Helen, a new neighbor whose children were grown. Helen offered to pray for Betty's family. An instant bond developed between the two, and Betty had no doubt that God had sent this friend to her.

At her church, Betty organized a ministry group in honor of her mother. The group is called Willing Partners. When they receive a call from someone who needs help, one of the group members arranges for the assistance needed. It might be a ride to the grocery store or a tutor for a struggling student. They have raked yards and mopped floors. Sometimes a caller only wants a prayer of encouragement. Betty feels that Willing Partners is a way to serve God and honor her mother's memory.

And this is the confidence that we have in him, that, if we ask any thing according to his will, he heareth us: And if we know that he hears us, whatsoever we ask, we know that we have the petitions that we desired.

1 John 5:14-15

CHAPTER 3

Lessons from Bluebell

Her latest coat of paint was a bright blue, making her chrome-framed headlights stand out. Parked outside of the McDonald's where my daughter Lisa worked, the little Chevrolet Vega appeared to be watching the comings and goings as if she had everything under control. She seemed to have an air of confidence about her that might say, "Don't worry! I've hauled around many a teenager, and I'm still going strong." I never worried that Bluebell would fail to get Lisa or me where we needed to go and back home again. Amazingly, even though she was old in "car years," she never had one break-down while she was with us.

Bluebell had come into our family under less than pleasant circumstances. My husband's business had failed, and my work barely brought in enough to pay the bills. The Ford I had driven for the past several years came to its demise at the top of an overpass in the middle of downtown. It wasn't going to budge another step – ever again. With existing funds, alternatives were few and far between.

I had written children's Sunday School materials for a Christian publishing company for a number of years. Recently I had given up that ministry because of the amount of time it required, and I felt my writing had become stale. Then there was a committee urging me to direct a women's Bible study group. I was planning to reject that position, because I didn't think my leadership skills were strong enough. I wanted to serve the Lord, but how could I stand before others when my life seemed to be on a downward slant? Our finances were pressing in, and now I was left without a car!

I bowed my head at the kitchen table. "What do You want from me, Lord? Are You trying to teach me something?" I wondered what I could possibly learn from this dismal situation.

Lisa bemoaned the fact that she would have to bum rides to her high school and church activities. Neither my husband nor I was thrilled at the idea of organizing our schedules so that he could take me to work and pick me up in the afternoon. The outlook added to my gloomy attitude.

However, in a short time God sent an unexpected blessing our way. A 1974 Vega had been bequeathed to our church by a family whose teenagers had driven it. That family had purchased it from a used car lot several years earlier. We were able to buy it for three hundred dollars to be paid out monthly, whenever we were able. It was just what we needed for the situation at hand. We ceremoniously christened the car Bluebell, and she became our friend and helper for many months to come.

Of course, there were some quirks associated with driving Bluebell, as with any older car. We had to pump the brake pedal twice before the car started to slow down. (The mechanic insisted this wasn't dangerous.) Then we had to avoid turning a hard left, so that the little whistle that came from somewhere under the hood didn't rise to its highest pitch. (The mechanic said it was nothing to worry about.)

Bluebell used a little more oil than other cars we had owned, and there was one flat tire when a nail somehow found its way into our driveway. But we considered those inconveniences small when compared to the service she rendered to our family.

Lisa was just at the age to begin driving, so she learned the basic skills - first on the school parking lot, then on back roads – and finally right smack on the overpass where the last car had died. Bluebell responded to every stage of the "driver education" with patience, performing each unexpected stop, swerve, and jerk like a trouper. After twenty years, Lisa insisted that driving Bluebell made her a safer and more skilled driver.

But, alas, the day came when we no longer needed Bluebell. My husband had been able to resurrect his business by merging with another company, allowing us to get back on our feet financially. And Lisa had carefully saved money from her job to make a down payment on a car of her own.

Bluebell still had plenty of miles left in her, and she had loads of experience in serving others. We remembered that she had come to us as a special blessing from God. "I think she would love to go to another family that needs a blessing," Lisa offered.

And so it was decided. We would locate a family who couldn't afford to buy a car, but whose lives would be greatly blessed by having one. Lisa and I delivered our little Bluebell to just such a family. They were overwhelmed and suggested a payout, but we knew this blessing was to be freely given. After Lisa explained the brake pedal and the little whistle, we drove home almost silently – until we passed MacDonald's.

The spot where Bluebell always sat was empty. Lisa reflected aloud, "I wonder if I'll ever drive another car that will be like a good friend to me."

Yes, God did answer my prayer. He taught me some important truths, using an unexpected means – Bluebell. She was a perfect example of true servanthood. She was available whenever and for whoever needed her. When her time with one area of service came to an end, she quietly moved on to the next opportunity. Even with a few quirks that made her less than ideal, she kept at it, never wavering in fortitude and loyalty. Bluebell wasn't the most attractive specimen around, but that didn't hold her back. She responded to our wishes without question.

Now I know I cannot do less when God calls my name.

CHAPTER 4

Intercessory Prayer

God is able to do all things, and sometimes He intervenes in ways we do not fully understand or expect. You may have felt led, as I have on occasion, to say a prayer for an unknown person you saw walking down the street. In all likelihood, you will never know how God answered your prayer. In such cases, we can only follow His leading and leave the results to Him. However, a special blessing came to my friend and me after we interceded on behalf of a person we had never met.

Sherry, a special prayer partner, came on the morning that The Dallas Morning News announced the arrest of a well-known professional athlete in our city. He was charged with disturbing the peace. The man had reportedly been running down the street hysterically shouting, "God, save me! God, save me!" When arrested, he was still sobbing loudly and begging for someone to help him find the Lord. He spent the night in jail, but was released the next day.

My friend shared her thoughts about the incident.

"Sounds like he was drunk, or maybe he just snapped. But could it be that he was truly searching?"

Neither of us knew him personally, but for some reason, we were both touched by his predicament. We lifted him up in prayer, asking God to meet the man at his point of need, whether it was mental, emotional, or spiritual.

The papers did not mention the situation again for almost a year. But then, an article appeared that filled in the blanks. The athlete had been besieged with stressful life situations in his recent past. He was admitted to a facility to help him learn to deal with his problems. Doctors said he had been on the verge of a nervous breakdown and had been behaving erratically for several weeks before the incident.

However, due to the publicity, a Christian witness had sought him out and led him to Christ. Subsequently, he had become a committed believer and was scheduled to give his testimony at a local church.

God had burdened our hearts, and perhaps the hearts of countless others, to pray for this public figure. I believe God was there at my kitchen table that day.

Again I say unto you, that if two of you shall agree
on earth as touching anything that they shall ask,
it shall be done for them of my Father which is in
heaven. For where two or three are gathered together
in my name, there am I in the midst of them.

Matthew 28:19 – 20

CHAPTER 5

The Rwanda Genocide

As Karan sat across the table from me and began to share her story, I inquired, "Do you feel great sadness when you to talk about the difficult times in your life?"

"Yes," she answered. "There was much sadness, but God walked with me through it all. I have many things to be thankful for."

In 1990 Karan and her husband Ocan took their four sons and moved from Uganda into the neighboring country of Rwanda. Ocan was originally from Rwanda, having been born into the Tutsi aristocracy, which afforded its members elitist social and economic standing. While Karan was not a Tutsi, her family was wealthy, and she was raised with servants at her beck and call. Both Karan and Ocan were raised in Christian families. As a teacher of economics at the university in Uganda, Ocan was happy to be offered a full professorship at a university in Rwanda.

Their new home was situated in a neighborhood populated by ambassadors, dignitaries and other affluent families. Like most privileged people, Karan and Ocan sent their children to expensive boarding schools when they were old enough. Joseph attended an elementary school, Alexander was in middle school, and Nathan was soon to graduate high school – all in different neighboring towns. Matthew was already studying at a university in another country.

On the political scene, the Hutu people, the ethnic majority in Rwanda, were spouting hate toward the ruling Tutsis. Tensions reached a peak in April of 1994 and, as Karan put it, "It was as if the whole world exploded!" Any Tutsi, any family of a Tutsi, or anyone who even associated with Tutsis was killed on sight by the raging Hutus. Many Tutsis fled the country. Others hid as best they could, but the genocide claimed over 800,000 lives in four months time.

Because the fighting broke out so suddenly, there was no time for Karan and Ocan to gather their family. Karan was at home, but Ocan managed to get away from the university, and rushed off to find their sons. At that point he disappeared. Ocan was never heard from again. It is assumed that he was killed while searching for his family.

For weeks and months Karan, now all alone, prayed and hoped that her husband and sons were alive. She huddled in her closet among the clothes each time the houses in her neighborhood were raided. Occasionally, the invaders looked in the closet and moved a few items of clothing, but she was never spotted. She lived in constant fear and unrelenting heartache.

The worst of the fighting came to an end, but the confusion and turmoil continued. There was pandemonium in the streets. Survivors were frantically searching for loved ones. There were still random killings every day. It was impossible to get information or leave messages at the embassy because of the throngs of people trying to be served.

Two years passed. Karan contacted every school and agency in Rwanda. She searched everywhere she could think of, but she was unable to locate anyone who knew what had happened to her family. The pain was almost unbearable. She described her grief as being "too deep to cry." Her body felt completely numb.

Eventually, Karan made the decision to return to Uganda. Her parents were no longer living, but she felt the need to go home. Having no access to money at this time, she joined a small group of other survivors and walked the three hundred miles to Kampala,

Uganda's capital. Once there, Karan found that the land and other property she had inherited from her father had been confiscated.

She was lonely and afraid, but she knew she must make a life for herself. Karan, who was fluent in English, decided the only safe haven for her would be in America. A friend of a friend agreed to provide housing for her in the United States until she could find a job. She left her contact information with the embassy in Kampala so that she could be reached, and with the help of the Red Cross, flew to New Jersey. Soon she found work as a live-in housekeeper.

Months later when she answered her phone, she heard, "Mommy, Mommy! You are alive! Is Daddy alive? What about my brothers? Mommy, I love you! Can I come to see you?" It was Alexander! It was unbelievable! Karan learned that the ambassador from India had rescued Alexander from his boarding school, along with his own son, when the genocide began. They had fled to India. Because of chaos existing in Rwanda, they had not been able to locate Karan's whereabouts earlier. Soon, Mother and son were joyfully reunited in America. It was December of 1998.

"Dear God!" Karan implored. "Is there hope for the others?"

Yes, yes, yes, there was hope! A few months later, Nathan, with the help of the family that had rescued him from his school, was able to track down his mother. And later, by crawling through mountains of red tape, discouragement, and frustration, Matthew, the eldest son, was also able to locate his mother and reunite with the family.

Karan and Alexander rejoiced and arranged a wonderful welcome for Nathan and Matthew. Karan's heart was overflowing, and she praised the Lord. But she continued to grieve and pray for the rest of her family. Where was Ocan? And where was her baby boy?

Months later a letter arrived from an acquaintance in Rwanda. Enclosed was a note written on a small scrap of paper:

"Mommy, I am alive. Are you alive? Is Daddy alive? Love, Joseph."

With heart racing, through tears of happiness, Karan called the number provided. Soon she was speaking with her youngest son, now thirteen years old. Although the family of a classmate had taken Joseph in when the war began, he was left behind when they fled the country. He bounced from family to family, finally living on the streets for almost two years. He was alone, confused, and hungry. He survived by hiding and sneaking around to scavenge for food. Finally, he recognized someone he knew from the old neighborhood and asked for help. When Karan met him at the plane and threw her arms around him, she was stunned by his frailness. It took weeks for her to nurse him back to health.

Only Ocan was never found.

As Karan finished her story, she whispered, "God gave my children back to me. All of them. God spared my children and brought them back to me. How can I ever thank Him enough?"

Today, three of the young men lead productive lives in America, not far from their mother. Matthew lives in Uganda with his wife and children. Karan and her American husband visit him every year.

Wherefore also we pray always for you, that
our God would count you worthy of this
calling, and fulfill all the good pleasure of his
goodness, and the work of faith with power.

2 Thessalonians 1:11

CHAPTER 6

A Mother's Blessing

Ten-year-old Lee sat across from me and shared the fact that he wanted to ask Jesus to come into his heart. When he was a preschooler, we had begun talking to him about God's love. As Lee grew older, he learned that God loves all of us so much that He sent Jesus, His only Son, to die on the cross, taking the punishment for our sins. The teaching he received in Sunday School added to his growing knowledge of God's plan for him.

I had never pushed Lee about making a decision to become a Christian, because I strongly believe that each person's salvation is between him and God. The Holy Spirit will convict and lead one to want a personal relationship with the Heavenly Father at just the right time. However, I had prayed that this moment would come in my son's life.

We bowed together, and Lee prayed simply and earnestly. He confessed that he was indeed a sinner and that he believed Jesus had taken his punishment on the cross. He asked the Lord to come into his life and be his Savior. He then expressed his desire for the Lord's help as he tried to follow God's teachings in the Bible.

Tears of happiness trickled down my cheeks as Lee and I talked about the significance of this experience. We agreed that this was the most important decision he would ever make.

His sincerity and innocence were beautiful, and I felt God smiling. We discussed his desire to be baptized, and we decided upon an appropriate time for him to profess his faith publicly. For a parent, there is no greater satisfaction.

Therefore I say unto you, What things soever ye desire, when ye pray, believe that ye receive them, and ye shall have them.

Mark 11:24

CHAPTER 7

One More Pair

My friend, Ron, sponsored several medical missionary trips to isolated tribes in South America. Because I was a prayer partner for the missionary teams, he shared many stories with me that showed God's provision and care.

After one particular trip, he sat with me at the table to relate the events that took place among the tribe they had just visited.

He had taken along Dr. James, an optometrist. The doctor had packed several suitcases full of glasses with various prescriptions. From experience, he could make an educated guess as to what prescriptions would be needed most often, and he took more of those. He also took many other prescriptions, hoping to meet whatever visual needs he found among the tribespeople.

Before and during the trip, the participants, as well as many friends, prayed they would be able to help the people see better and that their spirits would be opened to the story of God's love and sacrifice.

A clinic was set up in a tent amid a thick cloud of tree tops. The natives recognized Ron from a previous trip to their location, but they were leery of Dr. James and the strange equipment he brought. With encouragement from the interpreter, a few men and women entered the tent and examined the big "goggles." They checked out the eye charts, which had pictures of animals in different sizes rather than letters, since the tribe was illiterate.

Dr James showed several pairs of glasses to them and put a pair on one of the men who was called Sheka. Sheka could readily tell that his vision was changed by the lenses. The look of surprise on his face created some excitement in the group, and they all wanted to have a look. Eventually, Sheka agreed to sit in the chair and let Dr. James put the big goggles up to his eyes. Each time the lens was changed, Sheka nodded or shook his head to indicate his sight was better or worse. When he finally flashed a big smile and nodded excitedly, the doctor quickly determined the correct prescription and sent one of the aids to find it in their supply. When Sheka put on the new glasses he was ecstatic. He pointed to a mountain in the distance and exclaimed through the interpreter that he had never seen that far before.

A great many of the tribespeople followed suit and were fitted with close, if not precise, prescriptions that allowed them to have greatly improved sight. Some of them had such impaired vision that they might be considered legally blind. Dr. James had anticipated this might be true, so he had included a number of prescriptions that were strong enough to offer good vision to these patients.

As expected, one particular prescription was needed more prevalently than any of the others. Shortly after noon on the third day, one of the aids told Dr. James that there were no more glasses with that prescription. She suggested that if it came up again, he would have to use one that would be less effective but would still improve vision to some extent.

It was not very long before another person was found to need that exact prescription. The aids reminded Dr. James that they had run out of that one. He instructed them to go back to the suitcases and try to find one more pair, commenting that maybe one had been miscategorized during the packing process. They followed his instructions, and guess what happened! They found one more pair! An hour later, it happened again, and he insisted they search all the suit cases for one more pair. Again they found one more pair. Throughout the rest of the week the scenario played itself out over and over. Each time there was found to be one more pair. Not two pair or three pairs, but one more pair as needed.

As the team was closing shop on the final day, Ron noticed one of the last patients they had seen, one whose vision was so poor that it required the strongest prescription they had brought. She was standing just outside the tent with arms outstretched in front of her, and she was weeping. Ron stopped by her side to see if she needed help. She spoke to the interpreter through her sobs and said, "Look, I can see my hands!"

Hitherto have ye asked nothing in my name; ask, and ye shall receive, that your joy may be full.

John 16:24

CHAPTER 8

Her Father's Picture

Evelyn was a writer of children's Sunday school materials. Along with the stories from God's Word, she used Bible-learning activities and games in the lessons she wrote to help youngsters grow in their knowledge of the scriptures. When I was a new writer, she sat with me to provide some guidelines for creating Sunday School lessons for children.

Evelyn explained that Bible study for children is designed to lay foundations for the salvation experience when the Lord reveals Himself in a very personal way. Even very young children can learn that God loves them, that He can do miracles, and that He is always good. They learn that God wants them to obey their parents, to be kind to others, and always be truthful. They come to know that the Bible is God's Word and that stories from the Bible are true. Boys and girls can know many things about God before they actually know Him as Savior and Lord.

Evelyn presented a vivid example of laying foundations for a future personal relationship with the Heavenly Father. She told the story of Molly, whose father went away to war when she was a tiny baby. For the next few years Molly's mother kept a picture of her father in a visible place. She talked to Molly about how much her father loved her and what a good man he was. She read Molly the letters her father wrote to her. Molly had a smaller picture of him that she kept right beside her bed. She knew many things about her father before she met him for the first time.

Then one day he came home. When Molly saw him face to face, she immediately knew who he was. She ran to him and exclaimed, "Daddy, Daddy!"

Hopefully, we will take time to thank the Lord for teachers who had a part in teaching us about Jesus. And, when possible, we can personally express appreciation to someone who served and prayed in ways that prepared us for a personal relationship with the Father.

If you abide in me, and my words abide in you, you shall ask what you will, and it shall be done unto you.

John 15:7

CHAPTER 9

A Sincere Witness

The neighborhood we lived in during the years my own children were young was blessed with many playmates. It was a time when kids were allowed to play outdoors and around the block without fear of being snatched away by strangers. We knew all of our neighbors. Moms and dads often sat on the front porch in the evenings and socialized. It was a happy place to grow up.

Most families in the neighborhood attended church, and several of those families were Jewish.

One December my nine year old son asked his Jewish friend Larry why his family did not have a nativity scene in their house. Larry explained that his family did not believe Jesus was God's Son. They thought the Messiah was yet to come.

My son was shocked to learn that Jews do not accept Jesus as the Christ. He began to question me at length over a period of days about the differences in the two faiths. He was very concerned about his friend.

Several days later when I called the children in for supper after an afternoon of playing, he had a satisfied look on his face. He announced, "Larry is a Christian now." I was a little taken aback, but I said, "Really? When did that happen?"

"Today," he replied. "I wrestled him down on the ground and wouldn't let him up until he prayed and asked Jesus to be his Savior."

I stopped short and closed my eyes, trying to imagine what his mother would say when Larry told her of his "conversion experience." Right then I realized there were many things I needed to teach my children about being good witnesses for Jesus.

⇒⇐

Confess your faults to one another, and pray one for another, that you may be healed. The effectual fervent prayer of a righteous man availeth much.

James 5:15

⇒⇐

CHAPTER 10

You Can't Be Serious!

There was a day when my son Joel popped into the kitchen to "run something by me." He draped his muscular nineteen-year-old body on one chair and his legs on the chair next to him. My first thought was, "This has something to do with money." As it turned out, it wasn't that simple.

He casually announced his plans to be married the following week. Not so casually, I mentioned that I had not been aware of any serious relationship in his life. As the story unfolded, I found out that, although he and Tina had met just the week before, they were madly and hopelessly in love. And there was more. She was thirty-two and had three children - the eldest a thirteen year old son.

The decision at hand, as far as I could determine, was whether or not I would panic, scream, tell him how stupid he was acting, and generally turn him away from my table. Quickly deciding against that tactic, my next thought was, "If not that approach, then what?

Interesting, isn't it, the way some decisions that are so important must be made on the spur of the moment?

As I frantically sought God's wisdom, Joel began to remind me of all of his best qualities. His memory was suddenly limited to include only the wise choices he had made in his life. He talked about the secret desire he had to prove himself to be a man. He asked, "Mom, haven't you noticed how much more mature I am than the other guys my age?" He was too busy talking to wait for my reply.

The Lord was with me and heard my pleading heart. In my calmest voice, I suggested that perhaps it would be wise to postpone the wedding for two or three months just to get to know each other a little better. After all, he had not yet brought her home to meet the family!

"Shouldn't Dad and I have the privilege of meeting our future daughter-in-law before she actually becomes our daughter-in-law?" I asked. He was silent for an uncomfortable amount of time, looking at his hands. Then he got up, gave me a quick hug, and said he and Tina would think about it.

You probably know the rest of the story. In less than two months Tina was a memory, and Joel was back to his good old immature self, having fun with the guys.

Often when I am sleepless at night, I remember times when I needed on-the-spot assistance with one child or another. I wonder what tragedies were avoided because of God's intervention in such situations. Then I say "Thank you," once again.

———⟫⟪———

But they that wait upon the Lord shall renew
their strength; they shall mount up with wings
as eagles; they shall run, and not be weary;
and they shall walk, and not faint.

Isaiah 40:31

———⟫⟪———

CHAPTER 11

Connie's Story

October 14, 1972, began like any other Saturday for Connie, but it was filled with so many twists and turns that it became one of the worst days in her life, and yet the most blessed day in her life. She shared her story with me over coffee.

Connie and her friend Jackie had been asked to write a song for a local singing group. They were working on the composition in Connie's living room while Libby, Connie's six-year-old daughter, played with her friend Susan. Eventually, it became clear that in order to make any more progress with their composing, they would need a piano.

This is Connie's story in her own words:

"Since I had left my piano back home when I moved to California, Jackie suggested we rent a piano until we could get mine shipped. So we piled the kids into the car and went to rent a piano in downtown Los Angeles. After completing our mission we started the long drive home. Being cooped up in the car, the girls became rowdier and rowdier. Libby was even more hyper than usual, leading me to suggest that they both go and run off some of that energy as soon as we got home. While Jackie and I started to go inside, the girls headed out to play with the kids across the street.

We were on the porch, just about to go into the house, when we heard a sickening crash and turned to see Libby being tossed high into the air. I was so affected by the scene that I could not move or make a sound. I just stood there and watched as my airborne daughter crash-landed on the hood of the car that had hit her. Her small body then went flying down the street and smashed head-first into a parked car. As she fell to the pavement and rolled underneath the car, I regained movement and led the charge to her side.

"Everything seemed to be in slow motion as I moved toward Libby with Jackie close behind. Susan stood screaming hysterically nearby. All of the neighbors had come out of their houses and were gathering at the scene as Jackie and I bent down to look at Libby, lying under the parked car. She looked very white and very still. I could see that she had a large hematoma on her forehead, and blood trickled from her nose and ran down the side of her face. Jackie said we shouldn't move her with a head injury, but wait for the ambulance to come. My mind was not on injuries or ambulances. I had seen enough dead animals who had been hit by cars to know that my daughter was dead, and I did not know how I could stand it. Jackie knew it, too. She felt for a pulse…. Then, to distract me, she told me to go to the house for a blanket.

"Like a zombie, I went in, found a blanket in the hall closet, and started toward the door. A close friend and neighbor met me at the door and asked me how Libby was. I whispered quietly, 'Libby's dead.' She started screaming and I saw her fall forward as if she were trying to go through the wall to hide from the bad news.

"Her screams jolted me out of my inertia. 'No! This cannot be!' I rushed out into the street. Not caring that the entire neighborhood was watching and hearing, I got down on my knees beside the car and started crying out loud to God. 'God, I know that You are faithful, and You know I cannot bear this. Please, Father, don't take my daughter away from me! I can't stand to lose her. You know I can't, and I beg You to bring her back to me.' As I cried and bared my soul for the world to see, I heard Libby's voice from underneath the car asking, 'Mommy, is this a dream?'

"Later, Jackie shared with me that while I was inside getting the blanket, she had continued to try to find a pulse, but could not. That is proof to both of us that Libby had been killed and then restored to life by the amazing mercy of God.

"The miracle was not just the fact that Libby was living and breathing after I had seen her lifeless. There was also the change that took place within me! It was not the highly visible sort of conversion that is found in the saccharin fairy-tale endings spun by Hollywood on the big screen. My transformation was more subtle. It was not an ending at all, but another step of God's work in me, Connie Thane.

"Though still the imperfect human being with all my flaws intact, I have gained something invaluable – a greater sense of God that carries my faith to a higher level. It is the faith that enhances all of my senses and adds the technicolor, vista vision, and surround-sound to my life by constantly reminding me what a miracle we are living."

———⇒⇐———

If my people, who are called by my name, will humble
themselves and pray and seek my face and turn
from their wicked ways, then will I hear from heaven
and will forgive their sins and will heal their land.

1 Chronicles 7:14

———⇒⇐———

CHAPTER 12

A Gerbil Story

Let's face it, parenting teenagers is challenging, to say the least. Most of us pray for wisdom and leadership as we embark upon that often stressful time. Some teens, God bless 'em, seem to sail through those years without causing their parents too many gray hairs. But then there are those who seem to push, pull, sneak, defy, lie, backtalk, rebel and scream their way through the process of finding themselves. In the end, however, the vast majority remarkably turn into stable, upstanding adults, who contribute to society. But, sad to say, far too many make choices so devastating that their lives and the lives of their parents are damaged beyond repair. No matter which category your youngster fits into, there is no doubt you have searched for the right thing to say or do when conflicts arise.

Paul and his wife came to ask me to pray with them about Gina, their teenage daughter. She was being disrespectful and having angry outbursts. Her behavior was generally unacceptable. Sitting at the table together, we asked God for His wisdom, guidance and patience as they tried to maintain control of her.

Gina consistently wanted more freedom than her parents felt was wise. They held their ground as she argued for a later curfew and fewer limits on where and with whom she could go. Usually the family ended up in a huge row, whereupon Gina would loudly retreat to her room, slam the door and hibernate for a few hours, leaving the parents to pull themselves together as best they could.

Paul and his wife had the good sense to stand united on their rules, and they continued to pray that God would give them a tool that would help them reason with their daughter. First, they agreed that they would cease raising their voices when there was an argument. They would refuse to lapse into a power struggle with Gina, but rather show her by their conduct that they were in control. They also agreed they would say "I love you" to her more often, so that she could not question their devotion.

A few weeks after our meeting, I recalled something that I believed might be an answer to their prayers. I had attended a study where the Bible teacher, Victor Miller, shared the following story which illustrates that God sometimes says "No" to our prayer requests to protect us:

'Billy's gerbil tried its best to escape. The little animal burrowed into every corner and side of the cage, hoping for freedom. Billy could see what the gerbil could not see. The cat was lurking just outside the room ready to pounce if the gerbil was successful in his efforts. Billy knew that if the gerbil got out, it would be killed by the cat. Billy loved his little pet, so he made sure the cage was securely fastened keeping the gerbil from danger.'

Paul chose a time when the family was enjoying dinner together to share the story with Gina. Gina laughed at the cute little story. Then Paul pointed out that, like Billy with his gerbil and like God with His children, parents can often see dangers that teenagers have not yet been exposed to, and they want to protect the ones they love the most.

Amazingly, Gina was able to connect with the story. She said she would be willing to listen more carefully to her parents' advice. This is not to say that she never rolled her eyes again. And there were still arguments over the rules, but when the conversation began to heat up Paul would say, "Remember Billy and the gerbil." On all but a few occasions Gina would respond positively.

Of course, there is no one correct answer when it comes to dealing with teens. What might be helpful with one may have no effect on another. However, God is faithful, and He loves our children as much as we do. Parents who are secure in God's love and peace can rely on Him to provide the tools they need to get through those terribly wonderful years.

Think About It

Have I mentioned that we ate meals at the same table? Sometimes I wonder how I had time to cook, let alone hold a job, teach a Sunday School class and attend three or four soccer games every week, considering all that was going on at the kitchen table. You may be wondering the same thing about yourself, because God is in your kitchen, too.

PART 2

More Stories about God's
Goodness and Provision for
His Children

CHAPTER 13

Mr. Martin

There had been a time when Barbara's father was a pleasant man. Mr. Martin attended church with his family, made a comfortable living as a skilled carpenter, and was often helpful to people in the neighborhood. Mr. Martin was a hard worker.

He had always been a teetotaler, but that began to change when a friend suggested that having a glass of whiskey every evening would help him to "settle down and relax."

While some people handle moderate drinking without problems, Mr. Martin was one of those who never should have taken the first drink of alcohol. Within a short time, the glass of whiskey wasn't enough. It became two glasses, then three. In less than a year he was a full blown alcoholic, facing the same problems that most addicts deal with on a daily basis. His life was no longer his own; he was controlled by his addiction.

Predictably, his marriage deteriorated. His attendance at worship services dwindled as he began to view church members as a bunch of hypocrites. Thinking he could hide his drinking from the family, he found work in another city. For a while he drove home on the weekends, but those trips became fewer and farther between as time went on. Finally, his wife could no longer pretend there was a marriage, and she sought a divorce.

His talented hands began to shake. Woodwork that had once

been close to perfection was deemed unsatisfactory. He drifted from job to job. Fender benders left his car dented and scraped. After receiving more than one citation for "driving while intoxicated" his driver's license was revoked. He became increasingly bad tempered, and the continued abuse of his body took its toll on his health.

Though Barbara's sister moved to another state, the two of them continued to pray earnestly for their father to be healed from the disease of alcoholism. They reminded him of God's love and their love for him. At their urging he joined AA, but he had one relapse after another and finally refused to attend meetings. Eventually, the physical pain associated with long term alcohol consumption rendered him incapacitated. The day came when Mr. Martin's condition was such that he could no longer live alone. Barbara urged him to move in with her and her family. He refused that offer and chose to live in a nursing home.

Sadly, Mr. Martin's cantankerous ways did not change, but followed him into the new environment. Nurses and attendants found it difficult to establish a friendly relationship with him, although they continued to take care of his needs.

Barbara approached the Lord with three requests for her father's last days. First she prayed that, while his life had not reflected it in recent years, God would allow her to have assurance of his salvation. Then she asked that there would be an attendant in the nursing home who could look past his irritability and sincerely show love to him. And lastly, she prayed that she could be with him when the end of his life came.

One Sunday afternoon Barbara had Mr. Martin put into a wheelchair and took him outdoors into the spring sunshine. During their conversation, Barbara asked him about his relationship with the Lord. He shared with her about the time when, as a teenager, he had asked forgiveness for past sins, and trusted in God for forgiveness of future sins.

The next morning Barbara received a call from the attending doctor stating that her father would probably not live through the day. She hurried to be with him. As she stepped into his room, an attendant was changing his soiled sheets. With what little volume he could muster, Mr. Martin was ordering him out of the room in no uncertain terms and telling the poor fellow that he was a no good bum. The young man went right on with his work, patted Mr. Martin on the arm and said, "I love you, Mr. Martin, even when you are mean to me."

An hour later, as Barbara was bent over her father stroking his head, he lapsed into unconsciousness and quietly passed into eternity.

None of us can understand why God heals some, and lets others continue to suffer in this life. As for Barbara, she cherishes the memories of her dad as she knew him before the addiction changed his life. And she is especially thankful for God's gracious answers to her last three requests.

＝⋐

And whatsoever you shall ask in my name, that will
I do, that the Father may be glorified in the Son. If
you shall ask anything in my name, I will do it.

John 14:13-14

＝⋐

CHAPTER 14

Hawaiian Adventure

Phyllis graduated from the university with a degree in elementary education. She was excited when she landed her first teaching position in (are you kidding me!?) Honolulu, Hawaii! Most of her friends who were also education majors wondered why they, too, hadn't taken the high road by applying for jobs in exotic places, rather than in their home towns or places close by.

Phyllis was not one to miss out on anything that promised to be out of the ordinary. And Hawaii was definitely out of the ordinary for a girl from a small town in central Texas. She was always the adventurous one who was willing to latch on to a new idea or activity. That is, as long as it didn't compromise her strong faith in God and her commitment to serve Him. She expressed her feelings about it this way, "We're only young once, and now is the time to be bold. I know the Lord will use me whether I'm in Hawaii or Podunk. I'd just rather be used where there is a rainbow every day, and the beach is right around the corner."

The Hawaiian people proved to be just as special to Phyllis as the island they lived on, and she fell in love with them. In addition to her teaching, she found places of service in her church, and she ministered to the "beach people." She made a host of friends around the islands. She might have stayed there permanently, but her parents were getting older and needed more attention than she could provide from so far away.

Returning to Texas, Phyllis settled into a teaching position in Dallas. Now that she was "back home," she asked the Lord to fulfill her ultimate dream – to get married and have a family. Years passed, but Mr. Right didn't knock on her door. Although she was happy with her life – there were plenty of social activities – she kept one eye open for the one-and-only who would sweep her off her feet. However, as her fortieth year loomed on the horizon, it began to look like the single life might be God's plan for Phyllis.

Then, wow! Talk about answered prayer! A friend from Hawaii called about another friend from Hawaii who was moving to Dallas. Could Phyllis show him around and make him feel welcome in the states? As a matter of fact, she could. And she did. The two started spending more and more time together. (Now she knew why God had allowed her to live in Hawaii!) Not many months later, to no one's surprise, matrimony was in the air.

The wedding was lovely – in a charming garden surrounded by live greenery and white magnolias. In keeping with Phyllis's penchant for things out of the ordinary, the bridesmaids and groomsmen wore colorful leis, and Phyllis wore orchids in her hair. Friends rejoiced.

But don't think that the story ended there. Remember the rest of her prayer – the part about raising a family? It was as if the Lord said, "You want children? How about three in less than two years? Will that satisfy you?"

At age forty-one Phyllis produced her first-born, Daniel. Friends rejoiced again. Eighteen months later twins Victoria and Josephine made their appearance. Friends rejoiced once more.

One of her friends put it this way, "I am extremely happy for Phyllis, but I'm very grateful that God didn't choose to bless me at age 43 with three children under three!"

Isn't it wonderful how God knows what each of us needs and when we need it?

＝≡≡⩵

My voice shalt thou hear in the morning, O Lord;
in the morning will I direct my prayer unto thee.

Psalm 5:3

＝≡≡⩵

CHAPTER 15

All Day Every Day

Sara says that she doesn't know where to begin when remembering the numerous answers to prayer she has experienced. Her life is like that of many Christians in that prayer is a regular, spontaneous, habitual part of each day. As a school librarian, and with children of her own, she is continually focused on the needs of boys and girls. As parents we would all like to know there are teachers who lift their students up in prayer. Sara is one of those.

Many of the answers to prayer Sara has received could be described as spectacular. But then she remembers that the work of God is always spectacular, because only He can miraculously intercede in both the small things and in direst of circumstances.

Because her life is centered in the Lord, prayers come easily for Sara. Often they are spur-of-the-moment prayers, when she becomes aware of a problem. And then there are times when her prayers are heart wrenching and intense – those times when the need is great and emotions run high. Sometimes her conversations with God take place as she kneels before the Lord. Sometimes not.

Sara has not been immune from times when God answered her prayer with a "No." Two of those "No's" resulted in miscarriages. While she still doesn't understand why, time and her faith have brought her to an acceptance of those loses.

Praise and thanksgiving are also very much a part of Sara's

prayers. First of all, there are her two healthy children. After her daughter Tara was born, the two miscarriages caused her and her husband to question whether or not God intended for them to have other children. They prayed earnestly for a healthy baby and then, along came Tucker. However, there was a major problem – an ultrasound revealed a shadow on his kidney that caused grave concern to the doctors. Prayers were offered by family and friends. For two years Tucker was checked regularly. Finally, the day came when the urologist declared him completely healthy.

Sara had a melanoma on her ear several years later. It took three months to determine that the cancer had not spread and could be removed surgically. What a blessing!

Other praises include the survival of a loved one after triple bypass surgery and the removal of a cancerous kidney. And there is the child of a friend she and many others prayed for over a long period of time. God answered those prayers with complete healing.

Sara says, "I pray daily for a strong marriage, because I think the devil delights in divorce."

Does Sara's story mirror your own? If you are a praying person, you can relate to Sara. No doubt, you have had many similar life experiences. What a privilege to be able to lay our needs and cares upon Him! What happiness it brings as He answers our prayers! What peace is in our hearts when we know that He cares about each and every circumstance! What joy to know God is in control – all day every day!

———≡≡———

After this manner therefore pray: Our Father which art in heaven, Hallowed be thy name. Thy Kingdom come. Thy will be done in earth as it is in heaven.

Matthew 6:9-10

———≡≡———

CHAPTER 16

Get Thee Behind Me

Is there someone you know whom you would point out as being a pillar of the faith? Mr. Gatlin is one who fits that description in my mind. When I knew him, he was in his mid nineties, but was still regular in church attendance. And he was always ready to offer godly words to those who asked his opinion or advice. Even more importantly, he was a man of prayer. I can remember hearing him pray, asking the Lord to help him be sensitive to Satan's wiles so that he would not fall into sin.

In his younger days, Mr. Gatlin had served in several churches as Minister of Education. He was a Bible scholar, after years of theological study both in and out of seminaries. He had retired from full-time ministry a number of years before. However, he had never retired from teaching God's Word. Men and women of all ages still enjoyed his in-depth Bible lessons from the Old and New Testaments.

Mrs. Gatlin, his wife, was a great prayer warrior herself, although somewhat less scholarly than her husband. She also taught a Sunday School class, and she still played the piano. But her favorite role was that of social chairman. Could she ever plan a party! And please don't call her or her friends "old ladies." They preferred "girls."

In addition to their Bible class on Sunday mornings, the "girls" had regular get-togethers that they called "business meetings." They met at someone's home during the week, where there was always plenty of food and a great deal of chit-chat. The one time I inquired as to the business they conducted, I was told, "What the girls have to say stays with the girls." In all fairness, I should point out that they spent time in intercessory prayer each time they got together.

At the age of ninety-three, Mrs. Gatlin suffered a mild stroke. She spent a few days in the hospital before being sent to a rehabilitation facility that would help her regain full use of her right leg. When I visited her there, I found her playing the piano in the parlor, while many of the residents gathered around and sang the old hymns they loved. When she saw me she announced that she was doing fine, but had a few thoughts about God's plan for her. "I've never been sick in my life," she said. "Now why is God picking on me at this late date?" Truthfully, I couldn't answer that question.

They were a delightful pair, and they added their own special spice to the lives around them.

On a Sunday morning in mid December snow covered the ground and the temperature was near zero. The pastor had considered canceling the services, but decided against it. Sure enough, as the Bible study hour approached, there were only a few people in attendance. As I headed to my class, I saw Mr. Gatlin walking resolutely down the hallway. I exclaimed, "Mr. Gatlin! What are you doing here on a day like this? You should be at home snuggled up by a warm fire."

He turned to me with a look that was between a twinkle and an evil eye. He replied, "That's exactly what the Devil said to me this morning."

Sheepishly, I walked away.

＝

And it shall come to pass, that before they call, I will answer; and while they are yet speaking, I will hear.

Isaiah 65:24

＝

CHAPTER 17

It's a Boy!

Bob Johnson had traveled to New York City for a business conference with other oil company executives. It was his first trip to the Big Apple, and he was looking forward to seeing in "real life" the places and things he had only seen in pictures. Plans for sightseeing were in the works, but business must come first.

The conference was scheduled for 2:00 pm. Bob had time to check into the hotel and call his wife, Alice, to let her know he had arrived in the big city. She assured him that she and her Bible study group had prayed earlier in the day for his safety. And they had asked the Lord to use Bob in a special way while he was on his trip.

He grabbed a light lunch and headed to the skyscraper that housed the home office of his company. There would be two days of business discussions, training, and planning with thirty other CEOs from around the nation. He had previously chatted with a few of them on the phone, but this would be the first time all of them had met together face-to-face.

Allowing himself plenty of time to get there, Bob checked the address of the office building and wrote it down on a slip of paper. He told the cab driver where he was going and sat back for the ride. When the taxi stopped, Bob paid the driver and stepped out in unfamiliar territory. He looked around, but there were no skyscrapers nearby. He saw some large buildings, all right, but they were apartment dwellings – slightly run down and looking like they could use some exterior paint. Trash cans lined the sidewalks nearby. Somewhat befuddled, he reached into his pocket for the slip of paper.

Wouldn't you know? It was his own mistake! The address was 751, and he had told the cab driver 157. No big deal, thought Bob. It was only six blocks away. He would enjoy the walk. Bob set out on foot.

About a block ahead of him, he noticed a teenage girl running out of one of the buildings toward the street. She seemed to be trying to hail a cab. As he got closer, he saw that she was African American and that she was crying. He stopped and asked her if she needed help. She sobbed, "My sister is about to have her baby, and I can't get a cab to stop to take us to the hospital!"

Quickly changing into "action mode," Bob told her to go and bring her sister, and he would get a cab for her. Shortly, he stopped a taxi and waited for the two women to come. But they didn't come. Maybe she needs some help to get her sister to the car, he thought. Letting the cab go, he ran into the building just as a man was coming out. Bob asked him if he knew of a woman who was soon to deliver a child. "Oh, yeah," the man answered. "She lives up on three." Bob raced up the stairs, and soon he was on the third floor where he saw the teenage girl through an open door.

Her sister was on the bed, so far into labor that she couldn't walk. She was calling for someone to help, but the teenager was hysterically wringing her hands. Without a second thought, Bob went into the apartment barking orders. "Call 911, then bring me some towels and a pan of water!" (How he knew he needed towels and a pan of water, no one knows, since this was his first such experience.) There was no time for further orders, because the baby was well on its way. By that time the 911 operator had called an ambulance, and she was giving instructions to Bob on how to deliver the baby, cut the cord, etc. In a short time, Bob was cradling a tiny specimen of dark-skinned humanity that was loudly proclaiming his entrance into the world.

At this point, the ambulance attendants raced into the room and took over. They wrapped the baby boy in a blanket. Then Bob helped them get the baby, the mother, and her teenage sister down the stairs and into the ambulance. He watched as they started for the hospital with sirens screaming. Bob went back in to wash up and get his suit coat out of the apartment only to discover that the door had closed and locked. He looked at his watch. It was 2:40 pm.

Bob walked the rest of the way to the skyscraper where the meeting was already in session. As he entered, silence fell on the room and all eyes turned toward him. There he stood with tie askew, hair disheveled, and shirt splotched with blood. Apologetically he said to his boss, "Sorry I'm late."

The story he related sounded a little like the "my dog ate my homework" excuse, but his appearance backed him up. Besides, no one would have dreamed up a story like that! It was a great ice-breaker, and Bob received a standing ovation from his colleagues.

Back in his hotel room later that night, Bob called Alice. "How was your day?" she asked cheerfully.

Bob replied, "I think God answered your prayer – that He would use me in a special way today."

Call unto me, and I will answer thee, and show thee great and mighty things which thou knowest not.

Jeremiah 33:3

CHAPTER 18

Can You Hear Me Now?

I t is a privilege to be asked by a friend to pray for a special need in her life. Such a request is not taken lightly. I am careful not to say "Oh, yes, I will," and then forget about it.

However, there was an occasion when a friend seemed to feel that the louder prayers were offered, the more likely the Lord would hear and answer. I was caught in an uncomfortable situation when Elizabeth's husband called me from the hospital and asked me to come to her room and pray with her.

I found Elizabeth in a great deal of pain due to a blocked intestine. She had been given some medication that promised to lessen the pain to some extent, but at this point the severe throbbing was still raging through her body. Several family members and friends were in the room trying to comfort her, but, for some reason, she decided I was the one to verbalize her condition to God. I stood by her bed, took her hand and began to implore God to ease her pain and allow her to sleep. Suddenly, she interrupted my words and said, "Pray louder."

Now, in my heart I know that God can hear even whispered prayers, but for my friend, I raised the volume of my praying, continuing to intercede for her. Before I could complete the first sentence, she repeated her request in a louder tone.

"Pray louder!" I continued to beseech the Lord for cessation of pain, but in a slightly louder tone. "Not loud enough. Pray louder!!" This time it was a command! How could I refuse a friend in pain!? A few snickers were heard from others in the room.

She repeated her demand several times, her voice becoming louder and louder, and I kept praying louder and louder. Can you picture my predicament? Soon the snickers turned to laughter. The noise in the room prompted the nurses to come to the door to see if an emergency was developing.

As the state of affairs continued to accelerate, I began a secondary prayer in my mind asking God how I could get out of this very awkward position. I decided I should end the prayer abruptly by saying a loud "Amen." As I was about to do that, Elizabeth suddenly looked at me with an angelic smile. "It worked!" she exclaimed. "The pain has gone. God answers prayer." And she turned over and went to sleep.

Truthfully, I've never been sure if God answered my prayers because they were loud enough to get His attention, because the medicine kicked in, or because He took pity on me and delivered me from a highly embarrassing situation. In any case, I can't help but think the Lord was laughing as well.

＝≣＝

Ask, and it shall be given unto you; seek and you shall find; knock, and it shall be opened unto you.

Luke 11:9

＝≣＝

CHAPTER 19

Just Call Him "Slick"

The Prodigals' House is a thriving church in a small town in Kentucky. Many of the members consider themselves to be prodigals, like the younger son in Jesus' parable found in Luke 15. That is, their lives had once been characterized by rash and wasteful extravagance, but they were lovingly welcomed into the arms of the heavenly Father and a fellowship of believers who cared about helping each other. The congregation was aptly named by its pastor Dr. Morgan Gilkey, who was himself a prodigal for many years.

In high school Morgan was a better than average athlete. His grades were good, and he seemed to be headed for a productive life. He began to drink alcohol, in the belief that a few beers enhanced his athletic skills. After high school, he joined the military and was sent overseas, where he played basketball on an Air Force team. The drinking continued, and then he was introduced to drugs. While he liked the drugs for himself, he also found that he could bring in considerable cash by selling them. In addition, there was a definite "thrill of the deal" associated with making a sale and staying ahead of law enforcement. He managed to get away with this lifestyle during his four years in the Air Force and after he was honorably discharged and returned home. He was so good at it that he earned the nickname "Slick."

Morgan worked at several jobs to maintain appearances, all the while using drugs and trafficking. He planned to make enough money to retire in seven years, sit back, and enjoy the fruits of his labors. Drug deals were commonplace and usually went his way. But one of those deals went awry, and Morgan found himself serving a twenty year sentence for murder.

Drugs continued to be a way of life in prison, but "Slick" was still slick, and he was never caught. Although he was often high, Morgan gave a convincing performance of a model prisoner. His "good behavior" resulted in an early parole, and he was out on the streets again.

Several months later he began to have occasional weird thoughts about kicking the habits that were so much a part of him. He started to feel a strange desire to live on the up and up. He tried to brush it off, but it was strong enough that he decided to attend church one Sunday.

As he listened to the sermon he felt flush, and perspiration broke out on his brow. He left quickly after the service, but he couldn't stop thinking about that experience. Was God speaking to him, or was it only that he was nervous about being in church? The next week he decided to go back again just to see if the same thing happened. Not only did he feel flush and sweaty, but God's Word coming from the pulpit pounded into his head and heart. He knew he must respond. He fairly flew down the aisle to the altar. He professed his need for the Lord and prayed for forgiveness.

Spontaneously, he turned and spoke to the congregation. "Most of you know me. You know what I have been. You know that my life has been all about me. I am confessing before you that it is no longer about me. I will serve God. I will live for God. And if any of you see me doing anything that would dishonor the Lord, I want you to confront me about it. I've gotten away with too much for too long. Please hold me accountable."

From that day on Morgan couldn't get enough of the Bible. He read. He studied. He asked questions. He attended every Bible study group he could find. When there was an opportunity, he traveled in the state and out of state to Bible conferences, hungering for more and more of God's Word. With every tidbit of knowledge, Morgan grew closer to the Lord. He was amazed at the thrill he was receiving from this new life.

Even though he was still on parole, Morgan got permission to go into the local jail and teach the inmates what he had learned about God. Many of them still knew him as Slick, and seeing the change in his life was a powerful witness. One of those men asked Morgan to be his spokesman when he went to court to plead for leniency. Providentially, Morgan stood before the very judge who had sent him to prison years before. The man eyed him suspiciously as he spoke, but listened intently. The plea was so sincere and convincing that the judge granted the requested leniency.

The jail ministry expanded into state prisons, including the ones in which he had been confined. At the same time, Morgan was teaching a Bible class in the evenings. Then a church in a neighboring community lost its pastor, and they contacted Morgan about leading their congregation. He was still on parole and, in his own estimation, was less qualified than many others. But he followed the call into the pastorate where he served for a number of years. God blessed this ministry, as He continued to bless His beloved servant.

Through the years Morgan completed his college education, mostly online. He continued graduate studies, and eventually, he received a Doctor of Divinity degree. "Slick" Gilkey was now Dr. Morgan Gilkey.

Though he was involved with people from all walks of life, Morgan never lost his passion for the prodigals – those who were caught in the wasteful, fruitless world of addiction, petty crime, and lack of purpose – the "all about me" life. This passion led him to leave his secure position as pastor and start a new congregation that would be open to everyone, but would especially seek to minister to those who wished to turn from recklessness into peace.

With a few followers, Dr. Gilkey founded the Prodigals' House, meeting in a school. Miracles abounded, and God was glorified at each step of growth for the small congregation. When the school was no longer available, they converted an abandoned building into a meeting place. Later they met in the Lion's Club Hall.

Aside from the salvation of souls, the greatest miracle of all was about to unfold. As the church continued to grow, Dr. Gilkey and his flock prayed for a piece of property on which to erect a building that would serve as a permanent meeting place as well as a testament to God's great love and provision. A very large corner lot became available at a cost of $32,000. Negotiations with the elderly owner failed to yield a price that was within reach. But the church believed God intended that land for them. As they prayed earnestly, they circled the property time after time, claiming it for God's purposes.

When the owner died suddenly, her heirs put the property up for auction. The Prodigals' House opened the bidding at $5,000. The auctioneer continued to appeal to the crowd for a higher bid. But, unexplainably, there was no other bid. Finally, the auctioneer called out, "Sold!" The land was theirs! Dr. Gilkey and his flock praised the Lord for His goodness.

But that is not the end of the story. A man who was not a member of the church announced that he would like to have a part in the ministry, and he wrote a check for $2,000.

Knowing what God has done so far, can you picture in your wildest dreams the glorious structure that will one day preside over that $3,000 lot in a small town in Kentucky?

Be careful for nothing; but in everything by
prayer and supplication with thanksgiving let
your request be made known unto God.

Phillipians 4:6

CHAPTER 20

The Little Girl with the Hidden Voice

Those of us who work with children in school or church usually form strong bonds with our students. Occasionally there is a child who has a disability or a problem that needs extra attention, and teachers do their best to address the issue. Sometimes little ones with special needs slip through the cracks. Or maybe, even after receiving extra tutoring and encouragement, they make little or no progress in one area or another. But it is a joy when we see the fruits of our efforts, as students grow up and flourish in the world.

Recently I had a chance to meet up with Julie, now a college student. We hadn't had contact for a year or so, and we spent some time catching up. As we chatted, I remembered the many prayers that my friend Carol and I offered up on her behalf. Julie had been one of those who needed extra attention.

After her first year in school, I followed her progress closely until she went to high school, so we had talked often and knew each other well. But I had never told her what a blessing her life had been for my fellow teacher and me. I asked if she would like to know how God answered prayers that she didn't even know about. Of course, she was anxious to hear the story.

About five weeks after the beginning of the school year, I was asked to test certain first graders who had been recommended for reading intervention. Although most children can identify the letters of the alphabet before they enter first grade, these boys and girls had not shown evidence that they had this basic knowledge. They were already falling behind the other students. My program was designed to help them master reading readiness skills and catch up with their classmates.

When I went to Julie's class to take her to the testing room, her teacher warned me that I should not expect any results. She said Julie had not spoken a word to anyone since school began – not the teacher, not even another child.

Sure enough, when I placed three plastic letters of the alphabet in front her and asked her to name them, there was not a peep. I removed those letters and used three different ones. Nothing. Just as I was about to remove the letters from the table, I heard a tiny whisper, "That's B. That's C. That's O." Although I was stunned, I didn't allow myself to show surprise. We continued with the testing, and she named most of the alphabet. To this day I have no idea what caused her to speak to me when she had not let anyone else hear her voice.

When she returned to her class, she fell back into silence. I hurried to tell my friend Carol, a first grade teacher, what had happened. We added Julie to the list of children we had already begun to pray for. Each day the little girl came to my room, and we worked together in a one-on-one situation. She learned the names and sounds of all of the letters quickly, and then she began to put sounds together to make words. But she reverted to her silent behavior when she left my room.

A few weeks later, I decided to see how she would do in a small group of students who were at about the same level of achievement. I discovered that she wouldn't speak in front of the others if I asked her a direct question, but if I asked the group a question, she would wave her hand and answer in her little whisper. That showed me that there was some competitive spirit inside that little personality.

As the weeks passed, I learned other strategies that brought her a little further out of her shell of silence. Eventually, my friend

Carol came and sat in with the small group. Julie slowly began to speak in her presence. When she felt comfortable with Carol as well as the small group of children, we decided it was time to move her gradually into Carol's first grade classroom. At first she spoke only to Carol. Then she began to speak softly to another little girl who sat beside her. Slowly she opened up to the class.

Although Julie would never become one to "chat you up," toward the end of first grade, she took part in a puppet show where she whispered her lines right on cue.

When the story ended Julie's eyes were brimming with tears. She remembered being in my class and in Carol's, but nothing about the transitions that took place that year.

She said, "I had no idea. I wonder what would have happened to the little girl who wouldn't talk if God had not placed you and me together at the right time and the right place."

I replied, "I don't understand it all, but I am sure of one thing: I would have missed out on a very great blessing if God had not allowed me to be a part of this special miracle."

Pray you therefore the Lord of the harvest that
he will send forth labourers into his harvest.

Matthew 9:38

CHAPTER 21

Run, Gary, Run

Gary was raised in a Christian home. He was an only child, and his parents took him to church from the time he was an infant. Even as a small boy he showed an exceptional interest in the Bible stories he learned and what they meant. The story of Jesus' sacrifice on the cross for our sins touched him deeply. At the age of six, Gary prayed for forgiveness and asked Jesus to come into his life and be his Savior.

Always faithful in church attendance, Gary grew in understanding, knowledge, stature and favor with God and man. As a teenager he began to share his faith with his high school friends. During the lunch hour he often gathered a group together on the campus and led them in discussions of Bible passages and topics relating to spiritual growth.

Through the years Gary, as well as his parents, prayed for God's will in regard to the life choices he would make. While in high school that special girl came into his life, though he and Marta did not marry until they graduated from college. Now he loves to share with youth groups that he never kissed another girl.

Gary's abilities and interests led him to pursue a degree in engineering. Shortly after college, he and Marta married, and he landed a job in his chosen field. They settled into a near-perfect lifestyle. The family expanded with the birth of two children. Gary was an asset to his company, and rose to the position of project manager. The money was good. Both Gary and Marta were active in their church, as he taught a Sunday School class, and she was involved in the music ministry.

Then, lo and behold! Along came a still, small Voice. At age thirty-two, Gary began to sense that the Lord was speaking to him about the idea of full-time ministry – not just any ministry, but the preaching ministry. He spoke to God about it, "May I point out, Lord, that your timing is way off!? You should have told me this fifteen years ago!" With that said, Gary went right on with his regular routine and daily schedule. That is, until a few days later when, during his prayer time, the Voice spoke again. The impression was still the same, but with more intensity.

Half jokingly, he mentioned it to Marta. Her response was, "No way, Jose!"

That's a big relief, thought Gary. He felt that the Lord would have impressed Marta with the same idea if it were truly the Lord's voice speaking to him. Finally, he could relax. It was all a big mistake.

But… Marta changed her mind. A few days later, she lovingly told her husband, "If the Lord is leading you into full time ministry, that is what we will do."

As God's urging continued, Gary's resistance grew stronger. Like Jonah, he became a fugitive from God, trying to put the idea completely out of his mind. And, like Jonah, he felt God's tender, but firm, hand of discipline. Nights became long and sleepless. As he drove his car, he could focus on nothing but the still, small Voice. It was maddening!

Gary was actually getting irritated with God. Why was He trying to mess up a perfectly happy life? After all, both Gary and Marta were active in church. Wasn't that enough? He mentally listed every reason not to accept God's calling. Why should he give up a great job and the money that went with it? Marta would have to go to work if he pursued a seminary degree. He had no desire to start over. And besides, he had no experience in public speaking. It just didn't make sense. Gary tried to put the whole idea out of his mind. He even stopped praying. His own frustration spilled over to the family. He found himself being sharp-tongued and irritable. Communication with Marta and the children was tense. A year passed.

Finally, the day came when he could stand it no longer. Falling on his knees, he prayed, "Lord, I can't run any more. I give myself to you. I want to serve you. I want your will, not mine."

God was patiently waiting at the end of Gary's long run – waiting to give him the most amazing feeling of joy and peace; waiting with answers to all of the questions; waiting with plans to bring about a preaching ministry that would be used for many years to further God's Kingdom on earth.

God is good! All the time!

Now therefore, I pray thee, if I have found grace in thy sight, show me now thy way, that I may know thee, that I may find grace in thy sight.

Exodus 33:13

CHAPTER 22

A Forever Home

Like many teachers, Laura Cain falls in love with all of her students. Occasionally, one child pulls a little harder on the heart strings than the others because of special emotional needs or evidence of neglect. Such was the case several years ago when Missy entered Laura's class. The child was usually dirty, her hair often looked as if she had just gotten out of bed, and she did not have the things she needed in the way of supplies. Laura's heart broke as she wondered what Missy's home life must be like. She so wanted to take the little girl home with her. She and her husband made numerous inquiries about the possibility of adopting Missy, but it was not to be. There were issues at hand that could not be overcome. Then Missy's family moved away, suddenly and unexpectedly, before the end of the school year.

Laura and Jeff already had three beautiful children, but a seed had been planted in their hearts and minds. If not Missy, was there another child that needed a family just as much? The matter was not discussed again for several months, but Laura casually began viewing various adoption websites. Then she began sharing her feelings with two friends who had daughters that had been born in China. Hearing about the joys they had experienced, Laura was drawn to look more closely at that option. However, she realized that serious searching could not take place unless Jeff felt as she did about the possibility of adopting a child from China.

When she broached the subject with him, he agreed to pray about it. Several nights later Jeff came in late from work. Laura was already in bed when he sat down beside her and said, "Let's do this." She squealed with delight, but suddenly they both became quiet.

"Are you scared? Laura whispered.

"I'm terrified, aren't you?"

"Yes, I am, but I believe God is leading us, and I'm ready to follow."

The long journey had just begun, but God gave them reassurances along the way. They explored a number of websites, and looked at the faces of many beautiful oriental babies and children. Jeff was searching at work one day when he was strongly drawn to one particular child.

The information given by the orphanage about this little girl included her age – about three years old – and the fact that she had been abandoned as an infant. In addition, she was non-verbal, she was not walking, she was blind in one eye, and had a cataract on the other eye. Jeff could not understand why he was so attracted to this child who had such enormous needs, but incredibly he kept going back to her picture. At home, he was a little hesitant to share his feelings with his wife, but he slowly began to tell her about the little girl. As Laura listened intently to Jeff's description, her eyes widened in disbelief.

"Show me her picture, Jeff! Show me! Show me now!" Amazingly, it was the very same child that Laura had been drawn to the same day as she searched at home. From that moment, there was never a doubt that this was their child.

Jeff and Laura applied through the online agency and were put on a waiting list. Families already on the list would be able to select a child before it would be their turn. They prayed for God's will to be done, but they also prayed that their impressions were right, and the little girl would not be taken by another family. Within six weeks a call came from the agency, "You are next in line, and the child you prefer is still available."

Jeff and Laura broke the news to Griffin, 16, Emily 14, and Shepherd, 6. The family was overjoyed that they would have a new sister. They named her Addie.

It would be another year before they were able to bring her home. Since then, Addie has had two eye surgeries which have given her partial sight in the good eye. She has learned to feed herself, she walks, and she giggles. She loves to splash in the water and play with her brothers and sister. She has not yet spoken any words; her verbal communication consists of a few sounds. But Laura is certain that one day she will hear Addie say, "Mommy."

Oh, the love of God is richer than all the treasure of man!

Trust in the Lord with all thine heart, and lean
not unto thine own understanding. In all thy ways
acknowledge him, and He shall direct thy paths.

Provervbs 3:5-6.

CHAPTER 23

The Late Bloomer

While Melissa was growing up on a small farm, she learned to love Jesus. From a young age, she knew that He had a special plan for her life. She very much wanted to serve the Lord, but through the years, life got in the way.

It wasn't that she forgot about God or turned her back on Him. She continued to attend church, and she read her Bible now and again. But she got sidetracked by certain choices and experiences.

First of all, she married in her early teens. Being a wife meant she had to do her part in bringing in enough money for expenses. She managed to earn her GED (General Educational Development) at age 16, while working part time. Then after a few years, she found herself alone with a small son to support.

Melissa was aware that God had blessed her with a sharp mind, and she felt that, in order to make a good life for her son and herself, she needed a college education. Her ultimate dream was to become an attorney. Moving to Lexington, Kentucky, with her little boy, she found a job and began taking classes at The University of Kentucky. Immediately, she knew she had done the right thing. The subjects were not difficult that first year, and she thoroughly enjoyed getting back into a learning mode.

Even more than the education, Melissa wanted to regain a close relationship with the Lord. She had let the years, the hardships, and the responsibilities take away the joys of knowing and serving Him. She began to pray for God's guidance in finding a church that would provide sound, biblical teaching, and He lovingly led her to just the right one. In addition to participating in Bible study and worship activities, she joined a discipleship group that challenged her to greater spiritual growth. Then, faithful to His Word, God brought bountiful blessings into her life. She came to know other Christians, many of whom became her close friends. Then there were opportunities to minister to fellow students and to needy people in the community. Her son was learning about Jesus in Sunday School, and he made friends there.

A sermon Melissa heard at her church challenged her to tithe. She earned enough money to cover expenses, but she didn't see how she could start out at the beginning each month by giving ten per cent to the Lord. What if something came up that required cash? She didn't want to get strapped before the next pay check. She read Malachi 3:10 over and over: "Bring ye all the tithes into the storehouse, that there may be meat in mine house, and prove me now herewith, saith the Lord of hosts, if I will not open you the windows of heaven and pour you out a blessing, that there shall not be room enough to receive it."

The verse seemed to be saying, "Give it a try, and see if your life is blessed." And she did. Once again, God was true to His Word. Neither she nor her son ever missed a meal, and they always had what they needed. One more proof of His faithful provision for His children.

The next blessing came in the form of a Christian man. After dating for two years, Melissa and Rodney came to believe God had brought them together. When Melissa completed her second year at the University, they married and moved to Rodney's home town. They settled in, and the next year Melissa gave birth to a second son. She had a good job and a good life. She was happy, but she could not shake the feeling that God wanted to use her as an attorney.

Rodney agreed to lay the issue before the Lord, along with his wife. They prayed about it for months. Then God impressed both of them so strongly that, at age thirty-nine, Melissa quit her job and went back to school full time. She was facing two years to finish her undergraduate degree and three and a half years of law school.

It was often hard to stay with the plan. There were times when she wanted to give up. But Melissa's faith in God's purpose for her carried her through.

After she passed the bar exam, Melissa and another attorney established a law firm. They specialize in assisting the elderly with issues related to their livelihood, their pensions, and their care. She takes time away from her practice each year to participate in mission trips to foreign countries around the world where she shares God's love and testifies about His faithfulness to those who love and serve Him.

What a joy to know that God is not limited by time, space, age or any other earthly thing when He is ready to implement a special plan for one of His children.

Cast thy burden upon the Lord, and he shall sustain thee; he shall never suffer the righteous to be moved.

Psalm 55:22

PART THREE

Sharing with your book club or study group.

CHAPTER 24

Thoughts about Answers to Prayer

God answers the prayers of His children. He may answer "Yes," "No," or "Later." Personally, I have received each of those answers. When a prayer request is answered affirmatively, I am happy, grateful, or even ecstatic.

When the answer is "No," I am disappointed, and sometimes, I must admit, angry with God. But in most cases, subsequent developments have revealed that A. what I was seeking would not have been good for me or the person I prayed for, or B. God had another plan that was much better than mine.

Yet, there are No's that I still don't understand. I don't know why some of God's faithful servants die in the prime of life. I don't understand why there are children who are not healed when parents and friends have prayed earnestly. I don't understand why God allowed my twenty-two year old granddaughter to take her own life, just as she was about to enter law school. It's hard for me to accept many of the tragedies and disappointments that invariably come in life. God understands my grief and distress, and He is merciful enough to let me vent over them from time to time. Ultimately, however, I must exercise my faith and believe that God knows best.

Perhaps the most difficult scenario for me is learning to live with the prayers that have fallen into the "later" category. I have no doubt that God will answer those petitions, but He has not yet done so.

There are circumstances that I sincerely believe are God's will that have not materialized. And I have prayed for many years for certain persons to have a relationship with the Lord, and, as yet, that has not happened. I have come to realize that I must be persistent in those prayers, and rely on God's goodness, His wisdom, and His timing.

Remember the story of Zechariah and Elizabeth who were the parents of John the Baptist? The Bible tells us in Luke 1:7 that "they had no children because Elizabeth was barren; and they were both well along in years." Yet we know that at some point in time Zechariah had prayed for a child. Notice what the angel said in Luke 1:13: "Do not be afraid, Zechariah; your prayer has been heard. Your wife Elizabeth will bear you a son, and you are to give him the name John." Zechariah had assumed God said "no" to his request, but in fact the answer was "later."

Apparently God had delayed in answering Zechariah's prayer for a long time. Scripture doesn't say specifically what purpose God had for the delay, but we know that John needed to come into the world just prior to the birth of Jesus? Luke1:17: "And he will go before the Lord…to make ready a people prepared for the Lord." The timing of John's birth was perfect for the particular work God had for him to do.

King David wanted to build a temple for the Lord. God said his desire was a good one, but his prayer would not be answered in his lifetime. That blessing would belong to David's son Solomon.

Waiting is hard, especially when one has prayed a number of years for one thing. Believing that God is faithful can carry one through until an answer comes.

Having to accept that some answers to prayer may not come in our lifetime can be difficult. The temptation is to become discouraged and bitter or, perhaps, decide the answer will never come and quit praying. When I stop to realize that the desires of my heart are not dependent on my being present, I can let go and thank the Lord for what He will bring to pass, whether or not I live to see it.

The Bible teaches us to persevere in prayer and remain faithful to God's promises.

QUESTIONS FOR DISCUSSION

1. When did you first begin to pray? Did you follow someone's example, or did you reach out to God on your own?

2. Have you found healing from the grief of losing a loved one? Describe your journey.

3. Read Chapter 3 again. If you have learned spiritual lessons from an unexpected source, share it here.

4. Have you ever been disappointed when God answered your prayer with a "No" only to find that He had something better in store for you?

5. Have you prayed for a loved one or an acquaintance who was suffering from addiction? Have your prayers been answered yet?

6. Describe an experience in which you talked to God about an awkward or embarrassing situation, and you felt He was laughing with you.

7. Can you recall a time when God answered your prayers with a "Yes," but it came much later than you expected? God's timing was not the same as yours.

8. Describe someone you know who is a strong prayer warrior. How has he or she impacted your spiritual life?

9. If you have experienced a memorable answer to prayer, please feel free to share it with me at *hustongallery@bellsouth.net.*

ABOUT THE AUTHOR

Growing up in Waco, Texas, Sue Huston became a reader and a writer at an early age. However, for all of her love of the written word, she didn't share much of her own work until some years after graduating from Baylor University. Subsequently, she wrote Sunday School curriculum for a number of years. She wrote for magazines and spent some time as a newspaper journalist.

She served as Director of Children's Ministries and Minister of Education in churches in Texas and Kentucky. She worked in public education as a reading specialist. *I Know God is Alive; He's in My Kitchen* is her first published book.

Sue and her husband have five children and seven grandchildren.